The Walking To

The aim of this guide is ⸱ history and capabilities of Force Armament Museum. Use this guide as a supplement to the informational pedestals located near each of the aircraft exhibits. If it's raining and you forgot your umbrella, use it from the shelter of your car. All outdoor exhibits are accessible from the loop road around the museum.

There is a map of the Museum grounds in the center of the guidebook. Exhibits depicted on the map are identified and numbered for easy reference in the map key. To find an aircraft numerically, use the Table of Contents to the left of this page on the inside cover.

It doesn't matter in which order you visit the planes. Stroll the Museum any way you like. But do spend some time with these aircraft. The staff and volunteers of the Armament Museum have done a remarkable job restoring and displaying these rare engineering marvels. Please take the time to pay tribute to their handiwork.

About the Museum

The Air Force Armament Museum is the only museum in the world dedicated to the collection, preservation and exhibition of artifacts and memorabilia associated with Air Force armament and its platforms of delivery.

The museum was conceived and approved in 1974 but there was no suitable structure available on Eglin Air Force Base until 1976. In the spring of that year, an old Enlisted Club facility became available and the Armament Museum became a reality. To help fund and perpetuate the museum, the Air Force Armament Museum (AFAM) Foundation, a philanthropic non-profit organization, was established.

From 1976 through 1981, the artifact collection grew, and the Museum averaged nearly 80,000 visitors per year. But in 1981 the building housing the collection was condemned, and the museum closed that October.

The AFAM Foundation then began what became a lengthy effort to find a new home for the Armament Museum. By mid-1985, $1.2 million in private and corporate donations had been raised and construction of a new 28,000 square foot museum was underway. In November of the same year, the new museum was deeded to the United States Air Force and opened to the public. Attendance continues to grow, with a record 128,000 visitors in 2011.

Length: 52 ft, 11 in.
Height: 15 ft, 9 in.
Wingspan: 67 ft, 8 in.
Empty Weight: 20,000 lbs.
Max Speed: 300 mph.
Ceiling: 25,000 ft.

North American B-25 Mitchell

Unlike most combat aircraft, which are typically named for birds of prey or forces of nature, the B-25 is the only American military aircraft named after a specific person - pioneering aviator General Billy Mitchell.

Described as perhaps the most versatile aircraft of WWII, the B-25 was used for high- and low-level bombing, strafing, photoreconnaissance, submarine patrol, and even as a fighter. Originally intended for level bombing from medium altitudes, it was used extensively in the Pacific for bombing Japanese airfields from treetop level and for strafing and skip bombing enemy shipping. It was also the most heavily armed aircraft in the world. One version of the B-17J carried a massive 75mm cannon and thirteen .50-caliber guns, for a total of 14 forward-firing heavy machine guns.

North American Aviation designed its prototype B-25, called the NA-40B, as an attack bomber for sale to the British and French. When the company lost out to the Douglas A-20 Havoc in 1939, a modified version of the aircraft was submitted to the US Army Air Corps for evaluation as a medium bomber. As happened with the B-17 four years earlier, the B-25 prototype was destroyed in a crash during a test flight. But Army evaluators had seen enough, the aircraft was ordered into production, and the first five B-25s were delivered in February 1941. By the end of the war nearly 10,000 had been produced in several models.

The B-25's most famous role was a surprise retaliatory attack on Japan four months after Pearl Harbor. Sixteen 5-man crews trained in total secrecy at Eglin Field for the volunteer mission, to be led by one of the Army's premier fliers, Lt. Col. Jimmy Doolittle. The B-25 was chosen for its range, bomb capacity, and its recently proven ability to take off from an aircraft carrier at sea. A mock-up of the 300-ft deck of the *USS Hornet* was painted on Eglin's Field One runway for practice. To accommodate extra fuel tanks two of its heavy tail guns were replaced with broomsticks, painted black to fool the enemy. Two 20-cent strips of metal fashioned by Eglin craftsmen replaced the sophisticated Norden bombsight, which was useless at low altitudes. These were attached to the bomber's Plexiglas nose and calibrated for attacks from 1,500 feet.

On April 18, 1942 the *Hornet*, with 16 B-25Bs lashed to its deck, was spied by a Japanese patrol boat. Assuming the enemy craft had radioed a warning to the mainland, Doolittle ordered his men to launch the attack nearly 200 miles short of their intended position. The volunteers were well aware that with the added flight distance they would have to ditch their planes in enemy-occupied China.

All 16 B-25s took off successfully, with Doolittle himself in the lead. They bombed select industrial targets in five key cities, then crash-landed or bailed out, one-by-one, as their engines sputtered and failed. Eleven of the 80 "Doolittle Raiders" were killed or captured. Three of the captured men were later executed. Doolittle expected a court-martial for losing all his planes. Instead he returned home a hero, earning a Medal of Honor and the rank of brigadier general.

Only days before, the Japanese government had assured its people they were invincible from US attack. The successful raid left them stunned. Although it caused only minor physical damage, it forced the Japanese to recall many of their best forces for homeland defense, raised fears among their civilians, and caused morale to soar among Americans and their allies.

B-25Bs on board USS Hornet, *en route to Japan, April 1942 (US Air Force)*

The B-25 served some important non-combat roles during the war as well. Generals Eisenhower and Arnold both used a modified version of the B-25J as a staff transport. The E and F models of the B-25 were used to test wing de-icing technologies.

The B-25J on display at the Armament Museum was the very last B-25 in the Air Force inventory. It was presented as a gift to the cities of Valparaiso and Niceville in 1960 for their hospitality toward Doolittle and his men in 1942. The aircraft was displayed for many years in Niceville's Memorial Doolittle Park. In 1974 it was donated to the Museum and marked as the B-25B flown by Doolittle during his raid on Tokyo.

Sources: 3, 9, 24, 64, 66

Length: 74 ft, 9 in.
Height: 19 ft, 1 in.
Wingspan: 103 ft, 4 in.
Empty Weight: 36,000 lbs.
Max Speed: 287 mph.
Ceiling: 35,600 ft.

Boeing B-17 Flying Fortress

One of the most famous aircraft ever built, the B-17 has been described as "probably the most significant air weapon of its time." The first four-engine bomber in US history, the B-17 became the symbol of the US Army Air Forces' daylight precision bombing campaign against Germany during WWII. As one aviation historian has put it, "...in the pantheon of World War II bombers, the B-17 unquestionably occupies the top position in the public mind."

In 1934 the Army announced a competition to develop a multi-engine aircraft capable of carrying 2,000 pounds of bombs 2,000 miles at a speed of 200 mph. Boeing Aircraft gambled everything on their Model 299, a behemoth pulled by four 750-lb radial engines, and a fuselage bristling with five .50 caliber gun emplacements. Present for the prototype's maiden flight on July 28, 1935, a Seattle Times reporter declared, "Why, it's a flying fortress." An icon was born.

Boeing's audacious design was a winner from the moment it left Seattle's Boeing Field for performance trials in Ohio, flying nonstop at a record average speed of 232 mph. But just after taking off for its final test flight in October it stalled and crashed, killing two men, including its pilot, Major Ployer Hill, for whom today's Hill AFB is named. The crew had failed to disengage its elevator control locks prior to takeoff. This resulted in a standard procedure still used by all aircraft – the preflight checklist. Despite the crash, Air Corps leaders were impressed by the Boeing model and ordered 13 for further testing.

The B-17 was a recognizable symbol of the US military even before the war. Its speed and endurance were much touted in the press during demonstration flights as far away as Brazil, and it starred alongside Spencer Tracy and Clark Gable in the 1938 movie *Test Pilot*.

In December 1941 there were only 200 B-17s in existence. The few on hand in the Philippines became the first American aircraft in offensive action as they attacked Japanese ships off Luzon. Production now went into full swing. By war's end, 12,731 B-17s in seven models had been produced by three different companies: Boeing, Douglas and Lockheed-Vega. Of these, 4,750 were lost in action, many during massive bombing raids of German industrial targets consisting of hundreds of aircraft flying in formation.

The toughness of the Flying Fortress was legendary. "Thousands returned to base torn apart by bullets, cannon shells, and flak. This characteristic gave the B-17 a certain mystique, and air crews loved it." They loved it back home as well. The *Memphis Belle*, a B-17F, eventually toured 32 US cities on a mission to raise homeland morale and sell war bonds.

Of the 1.5 million metric tons of bombs dropped on Germany by US aircraft, 640,000 tons were dropped from B-17s. By the end of the war in Europe, B-17s had claimed 6,660 enemy aircraft, with an average of 25 planes shot down per 1,000 sorties. At the end of the war the B-17 was declared obsolete, but its fame only grew. After playing another starring role in a war movie, this time with Gregory Peck in 1949's *Twelve O'Clock High*, some began to call the B-17, somewhat derisively, the "Hollywood Bomber."

The crew of the Memphis Belle, 1940s (US Air Force)

The B-17G on display here was delivered to the USAAF on July 5, 1945, ten years to the day after Boeing issued its first press release on its B-17 prototype. It is one of the last B-17s in US colors to engage in wartime operations for the United States. These aircraft never saw combat in WWII, but were sent to Hawaii in June 1952 to form the Air Borne Early Warning Squadron One. In early 1953 this aircraft and two others provided airborne early warning support to the 7th Fleet during combat operations out of K3 Airbase in Pohang, Korea and NAS Atsugi, Japan.

This B-17G is depicted in the 96th Bombardment Group (BG) marking. The 96th BG was re-designated the 96th Air Base Wing (ABW) on March 15, 1994, here at Eglin AFB.

Sources: 2, 3, 4, 45, 64, 66

Length: 65 ft, 6 in.
Height: 15 ft, 6 in.
Wingspan: 64 ft.
Empty Weight: 27,000 lbs.
Max Speed: 570 mph.
Ceiling: 49,000 ft.

Martin B-57 Canberra

In 1950 the Air Force urgently needed a jet-powered tactical bomber to replace the aging, propeller-driven Douglas B-26 Invader. What they had in mind must be able to take off from unimproved airstrips at night in any weather, carrying either conventional or atomic weapons, and must fly twice as fast and twice as high as the B-26. It was to be put to use immediately in Korea, destroying enemy supply lines before they could reach the battlefield, and conducting high altitude reconnaissance.

Because of the urgency, the lengthy design and procurement process was dispensed with. Only existing aircraft would do. Five candidates were put to the test. All except one were too slow, too heavy, or too small for the range and bomb capacity required. The ultimate winner was Britain's first jet bomber, the English Electric Canberra. On its way to the fly-off competition in 1951 it became the first jet aircraft to fly nonstop across the Atlantic Ocean without refueling.

With the addition of more powerful J65 engines, wing tip tanks, tandem seating under a bubble canopy, and a rotating bomb-bay door that reduced the drag of conventional doors, the British Canberra became the American B-57, manufactured under license in the US by the Glenn L. Martin Company.

The B-57 did not fly until July 20, 1953, just seven days before the Korean War ended. During the Cold War many were converted to the EB-57 electronic reconnaissance configuration and were put to use flying mock aggressor missions against ground-based early warning radar sites in the US, using electronic jamming equipment and chaff dispensers to jam friendly radar during training missions. They were often painted glossy black to evade detection from the ground.

This aircraft came off the assembly line in 1955 and was one of only 22 B models to be converted to the EB-57 electronic reconnaissance configuration. It was converted back to a medium bomber in 1967 and served for two years in Vietnam, finally returning stateside to serve in the Air National Guard. Dropped from the AF inventory in 1972, it was obtained by the Armament Museum in 1991.

Sources: 2, 3, 11, 48, 66, 69

Length: 96 ft, 10 in.
Height: 38 ft, 6 in.
Wingspan: 132 ft, 7 in.
Empty Weight: 69,300 lbs.
Max Speed: 380 mph.
Ceiling: 33,000 ft.

Lockheed AC-130 Spectre

The Armament Museum's AC-130 Hercules was the very first one produced and delivered to the US Air Force in 1955. In a later incarnation, in 1967, it was one of the first seven C-130s to be transformed into the Army's newest secret weapon in Vietnam, the AC-130A Spectre gunship. Affectionately dubbed *First Lady* by its crew, this aircraft is truly an historic gem.

The *First Lady* came off the Lockheed assembly line on March 10, 1955. It was the first US plane to use the new turboprop propulsion technology, which powered the propeller by using the heat of combustion to turn a turbine rather than a series of pistons. Much larger than earlier transports like the C-47 Spooky, the C-130 Hercules could accommodate 92 combat troops and their gear, or up to 45,000 pounds of cargo. It had an upswept rear fuselage with the floor serving as the loading ramp, and tricycle landing gear designed for short, bumpy airfields. Over its long career, the Hercules has been used to refuel helicopters in flight, to transport the wounded from battle, to track and recover satellites and space capsules, and to study weather phenomena. It has been used for aerial photo and electronic surveillance and Coast Guard search and rescue operations. Outfitted with skis, it has supplied Antarctic research bases. The C-130 has been so successful that later models are still in service around the world, more than 50 years after their introduction.

By the mid 1960s the effectiveness of the AC-47 gunship to support ground troops in Vietnam had already been proven. But it was soon obvious that bigger guns were needed, along with a bigger airplane that could shoot more rounds with more accuracy from safer altitudes. With its high-wing design and large ammo-carrying capacity, the Hercules was the perfect choice. Gun ports could be placed under the wings for unobstructed access to targets, and a formidable array of armament was now possible. In the spring of 1967 the Air Force retrofitted a 10-year-old C-130 with four 7.62mm miniguns and four M61 20mm Vulcan cannons. It was also equipped with the latest targeting technology, including infrared cameras, side-looking radar, and night vision. With a potential firepower of 11,200 rounds per minute, the old cargo plane had become a veritable "flying tank."

The first AC-130A Spectre gunship was flight tested at Eglin AFB over the summer of 1967. In September it was sent to Southeast Asia for combat testing. In the meantime, six additional AC-130As were produced in the US for service in Vietnam, including the *First Lady*. These entered combat in 1968. Spectre gunships served until the end of the Vietnam conflict, destroying more than 10,000 enemy trucks and conducting many life-saving close air support missions. Its performance earned it the nickname the "Four Engine Fighter."

Enemy antiaircraft artillery (AAA) exacted a heavy toll on the gunships during their first months in combat. In 1969 an exploding 37mm shell sheered the *First Lady's* nose off and destroyed everything below the crew deck. Fortunately, she was repaired and continued in service for another 26 years. The use of F-4 Phantom escorts took care of much of the AAA problem in the last few years of the war.

AC-130H Spectre jettisons flares (US Air Force)

In July 1975 all remaining AC-130As became part of the 711th Special Operations Squadron at Duke Field, Eglin AFB, the only gunship unit in the Air Force Reserve, and the only unit, active or Reserve, owning and flying the A-Model gunships.

AC-130 gunships have played a crucial role in every major combat engagement since Vietnam. There are 25 AC-130s currently active as part of Operation Enduring Freedom. Seventeen of these are the new AC-130U Spooky, owned by the 16th Special Operations Squadron at Hurlburt Field, Florida.

After 40 years and nearly 14,000 flight hours of service, the *First Lady* was retired on Sept 10, 1995 along with the other four remaining A-Model gunships, in a ceremony at Hurlburt Field. After seeing the *First Lady* at an air show a few years earlier, King Hussein of Jordan had offered to buy her. Instead, after one final live fire demonstration over Eglin's Range A-77, she was put on permanent static display at the AF Armament Museum.

Sources: 2, 3, 17, 55, 66

Length: 53 ft, 4 in.
Height: 14 ft, 8 in.
Wingspan: 57 ft, 6 in.
Empty Weight: 25,000 lbs.
Max Speed: 450 mph.
Ceiling: 45,000 ft.

Fairchild Republic A-10 Thunderbolt II

With a fuselage built around a two-ton, 20-foot-long Gatling gun, under-wings bristling with Maverick missiles, and a cockpit encased in a "bathtub" of 1.5-inch-thick titanium armor, it's not surprising the A-10 is nicknamed the "Warthog." As one writer has put it, "the name was too appropriate not to stick to an ugly beast with a thick hide and dangerous tusks."

The A-10's design was driven by an urgent need for a dedicated close air support (CAS) aircraft to attack hostile ground forces on the battlefront in Vietnam, and to protect Europe from a possible Soviet invasion. Envisioned was an aircraft that could take off from primitive airfields carrying a large load of tank-killing ordnance, loiter "on call" near the battlefront for hours, maneuver in slow, tight turns to engage the enemy, and return to base, scarred but intact, for quick repairs.

Fairchild Republic delivered the first A-10 to the Air Force in 1975. With two turbofan engines attached high on the rear fuselage, a twin tail, broad, straight wings set low on the fuselage, and long, spindly legs, it was unlike anything ever seen before. But it's what couldn't be seen that really made the A-10 remarkable. Hidden inside the fuselage was a massive, seven-barrel GAU-8 rotary cannon capable of firing 30mm armor-piercing projectiles at 4,200 rounds per minute. Also hidden were 1,200 lbs of titanium armor plating, and triple-redundant flight control systems designed to allow the plane to return safely to base with failed hydraulics and half a wing shot off. Fully armed, a single Warthog was capable of taking out a dozen main battle tanks.

During the 1991 Gulf War, A-10s destroyed more than 1,000 Iraqi tanks, 1,200 artillery pieces, and 2,000 other military vehicles. Warthogs were used in Bosnia and Kosovo during the 1990s, in Iraq and Afghanistan during the War on Terror, and in 2011 were deployed as part of Operation Odyssey Dawn, the coalition intervention in Libya. It is expected to continue its CAS role until at least 2028.

The Armament Museum's A-10 was manufactured in 1977 and has been part of the Museum's inventory since 2001.

Sources: 1, 3, 19, 66, 75, 79

Length: 49 ft, 5 in.
Height: 16 ft.
Wingspan: 32 ft, 8 in.
Empty Weight: 19,100 lbs.
Max Speed: 1,500 mph.
Ceiling: 50,000 ft.

General Dynamics F-16 Fighting Falcon

Small, quick, and highly maneuverable, the F-16 has dominated the US Air Force's fighter fleet for more than three decades. The powerful turbofan engine of the F-16 exerts a thrust equal to the weight of the aircraft. This means it is capable of phenomenal acceleration. Strapped into a seat reclined 30 degrees to maintain consciousness during 9-G turns, the F-16 pilot uses computerized fly-by-wire controls to outmaneuver his opponents in dogfights, decelerating so rapidly that the chasing enemy becomes the chased. Pilots love their F-16s. Its official moniker, "Fighting Falcon," never caught on. To the F-16 pilot it's a "Viper," named after the indomitable fighters in *Battlestar Galactica*.

The F-16 was developed by General Dynamics in the early 1970s as part of the Lightweight Fighter (LWF) program. Ever since the P-51 Mustang of WWII, each new US fighter had cost more than twice as much as its predecessor. The fear of Soviet numerical superiority in the air called for a shift in thinking. The idea behind the LWF competition was to augment the expensive F-15 Eagle with a cheaper, high-performance alternative that could be built in quantity. Since its introduction in 1978 the Fighting Falcon has been adopted by more than 20 allied nations.

Originally designed as a daytime air-to-air fighter, the Viper has been adapted successfully to multiple roles, including night precision strike, suppression of enemy defenses, photoreconnaissance, close air support, and forward air control. But its reputation as the world's top dogfighter remains unsurpassed. In 1981 Israeli F-16 pilots shot down 44 Syrian MiGs without a single loss. During the 1991 Gulf War F-16s flew more missions than any other aircraft, destroying Iraqi airfields and Scud missile launch sites.

The US Air Force aerial demonstration team, the Thunderbirds, have been flying F-16s since 1983.

Despite a shift in US fighter procurement to the new F-35 Lightning II, Lockheed Martin (which bought General Dynamics' aircraft division in 1993) is still producing F-16s at its Fort Worth plant for foreign customers, and hopes to continue for several more years. To date approximately 4500 F-16s have been produced worldwide.

Sources: 2, 3, 5, 23, 30, 41, 54, 66, 71

Length: 63 ft, 9 in.
Height: 18 ft, 6 in.
Wingspan: 42 ft, 10 in.
Empty Weight: 31,700 lbs.
Max Speed: 1,600 mph.
Ceiling: 65,000 ft.

McDonnell Douglas F-15 Eagle

With a combat record of more than 100 victories and zero losses, the F-15 Eagle is the world's most successful fighter. And with the demise of the F-22 Raptor program and delays in fielding the F-35 Joint Strike Fighter, it seems the Eagle will continue to soar for some time to come.

The key to its success is low wing-loading (the ratio of weight to wing area) combined with a high thrust-to-weight ratio (meaning the thrust from its twin turbofans is greater than the weight of the aircraft). The F-15 can take off and land at low speeds on short runways, accelerate faster than any of its adversaries, perform tight, high-g turns without losing airspeed, and reach supersonic speeds in a vertical climb, like a rocket launching into space.

The development of the F-15 was a response to the appearance of sophisticated new Soviet MiG fighters in the late 1960s that the Pentagon feared could render the F-4 Phantom obsolete. Until now, conventional thinking had been that one-on-one aerial dogfights were a thing of the past. Not since the Korean War-era F-86 Sabre had the US fielded a jet designed especially for this role -- an air-superiority fighter. Spurred by the Soviet threat, the Air Force sponsored an industry design competition that called for a long-range tactical air-superiority fighter that could destroy enemy aircraft at a great distance ("beyond visual range"), but could also defeat its opponents in close-in aerial combat.

McDonnell Douglas won the competition in 1969, and the F-15 Eagle made its first flight in 1972. Deliveries to combat units began in 1975. Israel was the first export customer for the F-15, and the first to use it in combat. Since then the air forces of Saudi Arabia, Japan and South Korea have likewise adopted the Eagle as their primary air-superiority fighter.

The United States first used the F-15 in combat in the 1991 Gulf War, destroying 32 Iraqi jets in aerial combat. Twelve years later, in the 2003 Iraq War, the Iraqi air force wisely chose to remain grounded rather than take on American Eagle pilots.

Sources: 2, 3, 26, 30, 31, 66, 89

Length: 64 ft, 5 in.
Height: 16 ft, 11 in.
Wingspan: 95 ft.
Empty Weight: 17,000 lbs.
Max Speed: 232 mph.
Ceiling: 25,000 ft.

Douglas AC-47 Spooky

The Douglas AC-47 (the "AC" stands for Attack Cargo) was a new, Vietnam-era configuration of an old WWII workhorse - the versatile C-47 Skytrain, or "Gooney Bird." The Gooney Bird itself was, in turn, a military adaptation of the pre-World War II DC-3 commercial airliner, first flown in 1935.

The 21-passenger DC-3 had revolutionized commercial air travel in the late 1930s. A "sleeper" version of the plane had berths for 14 overnight passengers. For the first time in history, a traveler could leave New York before dinner, get a good night's sleep, and arrive fresh to work in the morning – in Los Angeles. By 1940, with international sales surging, the Douglas DC-3 had captured more than 80 percent of the world's civilian air traffic.

With the outbreak of WWII, the US government halted the construction of commercial DC-3s and ordered Douglas to mass-produce a military version that could be used to carry personnel or cargo, tow troop-carrying gliders, drop paratroopers, or evacuate wounded soldiers from the combat zone. Many of the soldiers who parachuted into Normandy on D-Day, did so from C-47s. From 1940 until the end of the war six years later, more than 10,000 C-47s were built. At one point during the war, US factories were cranking out nearly two per hour.

Two decades and two wars later, the situation in Vietnam demanded an aircraft that could supplement fighters for close air support of ground troops. The Army needed a platform that could fly slowly and at low elevations, but also had the ability to stay in the air for hours while carrying a heavy load of flares, spotlights, and ammunition. A cargo plane was the only type of vehicle meeting all the requirements. The C-47 was the chosen aircraft. With a few modifications, including the installation of three .30-caliber machine guns poking out of the left side of the fuselage, the new "gunships" were hurriedly tested at Eglin AFB. By December 1964 the first AC-47 was tested in combat from Bien Hoa Air Base, South Vietnam.

The gunship proved to be very successful in breaking up enemy attacks on small villages and other defensive positions. Within a year, a couple dozen rehabilitated Gooney Birds, now armed with 7.62mm SUU-11A Gatling-style Miniguns, and with the call-sign "Spooky," joined the Vietnam conflict as part of the 4th Air Commando Squadron.

A typical night mission included a crew of seven, plus an assigned Vietnamese "observer" who assisted the navigator. The underside of the aircraft was painted black to blend into the night sky, while the upper portions were jungle camouflage. Floating along at less than 130 mph, at an elevation below 3000 feet, the pilot signaled for the loadmaster to drop MK-24 flares, which illuminated the target area with 2 million candlepower for up to three minutes at a time. Approaching the target, the pilot rolled into a 30-degree banked left turn, sighted the target with his heads-up display, and fired 3-second bursts with his Miniguns. At 6,000 rounds per minute, the rotating Gatlings placed a bullet every 2.4 yards over a 52-yard area every three seconds. Having never seen such a display of firepower so close to the ground - in the dark - the Viet Cong likened the AC-47 to a fire-breathing dragon. Picking up on the theme, the crews of the Spooky began to use another nickname for their aircraft: Puff the Magic Dragon.

Loading ammunition into an AC-47 Spooky (US Air Force)

Of the thousands of C-47s produced by the US, only 53 were modified into AC-47 gunships. The majority of those that survived were turned over to the South Vietnamese Air Force in 1969 as more durable AC-130s and AC-119s took over the close air support function.

The C-47 on display at the Armament Museum was built in March 1945, and spent its entire active life stateside. By 1966 it was one of only thirty C-47s left in the Army inventory. It was procured by the National Museum of the United States Air Force and shipped to the Armament Museum for static display in October 1976. It is painted and marked as an AC-47 assigned to the 4th Special Operations Squadron, 14th Special Operations Wing, Udorn Royal Thai AFB, during the Vietnam War from 1969-1970.

Sources: 2, 3, 57, 66

Length: 73 ft, 6 in.
Height: 17 ft, 6 in.
Wingspan: 63 ft. extended
Empty Weight: 46,170 lbs.
Max Speed: 1,452 mph.
Ceiling: 57,000 ft.

General Dynamics F-111 Aardvark

Nicknamed for its long, straight nose, the Aardvark's path to production was equally long, and decidedly more tortuous. During bitter fights in Congress and between the Navy and Air Force over its development, the plane that started out as the Defense Secretary's pet project became the bane of Capitol Hill (dubbed "McNamara's flying Edsel"), but it would eventually prove to be one of the most effective fighting machines ever built.

The controversy started in 1960 with a call to industry to design an aircraft that could do it all – close air support, long-range bombing, air-to-air combat – for both the Air Force and the Navy. As the program struggled through the 1960s, a succession of painful compromises were struck, and neither service got what it wanted. The Navy finally backed out altogether. The Air Force sent its first six F-111As to Vietnam in 1968 to replace its aging fleet of F-105 Thunderchiefs. Within weeks, half the F-111s were lost due to structural defects. The Aardvark was sent back home, and its manufacturer, General Dynamics, was ordered back to the drawing board.

In 1972 the F-111 finally proved itself in Vietnam, striking targets in weather that grounded all other aircraft, the terrain-following radar in its nosecone sniffing the contours of the hilltops only 200 feet below. Its technology was groundbreaking. The F-111 could fly nonstop across the Atlantic, a formation of four carrying the bomb load of twenty F-4s. The first aircraft with "swing wings," it could take off from unimproved runways, sweep its wings rearward, and accelerate to Mach 2.5. Its crew sat side-by-side in a watertight crew capsule that could be jettisoned in flight and float safely to the ground.

In 1986 the Aardvark achieved lasting fame when eighteen of them flew from England to Libya and back, a flight of 6,400 miles, and unloaded their bomb bays on Qaddafi's Tripoli, in the longest fighter combat mission in history. During the Gulf War, F-111s were invaluable in night raids against Iraqi tanks, flying 4,000 sorties without a single loss.

The museum's F-111E was manufactured in 1971 and has been on display since 1992.

Sources: 2, 3, 12, 30, 66

Length: 62 ft, 10 in.
Height: 16 ft, 6 in.
Wingspan: 38 ft, 5 in.
Empty Weight: 28,275 lbs.
Max Speed: 1,384 mph.
Ceiling: 55,200 ft.

McDonnell Douglas RF-4 Phantom II

A reconnaissance version of Vietnam's premier fighter jet, the McDonnell Aircraft RF-4 Phantom II served the US Air Force for more than three decades, from the beginning of Vietnam through the Gulf War. The RF-4 was nearly identical to its fighting counterpart. It had the same powerful twin turbojets, capable of propelling the 25-ton aircraft beyond Mach 2, and the same unorthodox appearance, earning the F-4 such nicknames as "Double Ugly," "The Flying Anvil," and "Iron Pig." What made the RF-4 different from the F-4 is that it carried cameras instead of missiles.

Enemy aerial reconnaissance during the early years of the Vietnam conflict was handled in large part by the RF-101 Voodoo. The Voodoo was fast, but with its specialized equipment it was not quite fast enough to keep its distance from an increasing presence of North Vietnamese MiGs. The Air Force began the development of a reconnaissance version of the Navy's F-4 Phantom II at the same time as it was developing its F-4C air superiority fighter. Beginning in 1965 both versions of the Phantom were produced in great numbers and shipped off to the combat zone. The RF-4C had largely replaced the Voodoo in the tactical reconnaissance role by 1970.

With a fuselage nearly five feet longer than the F-4, the RF-4 could accommodate a variety of cameras in its nose section. Its gigantic HIAC-1 LOROP (Long Range Oblique Photography) camera, suspended in an underbelly pod, was capable of taking high-resolution images of objects up to 100 miles away. Terrain-following radar allowed the aircraft to fly at high speeds just above the treetops, automatically maintaining a constant altitude above the ground surface. Infrared viewers could detect enemy ground forces in pitch darkness.

The Armament Museum's RF-4C was built in 1968 and served during the war with the 460th Tactical Reconnaissance Wing (Pacific Air Force) at Tan Son Nhut Airbase, South Vietnam, and at Kadena Airbase, Korea. In 1971 she was deployed to Ramstein and Solingen Air Bases, Germany with the 67th Tactical Reconnaissance Wing (TAC). She was assigned to Eglin AFB in 1977 and went on static display in 1995.

Sources: 3, 66, 72

Length: 42 ft, 7 in.
Height: 12 ft, 8 in.
Rotor Diameter: 44 ft.
Empty Weight: 4,750 lbs.
Max Speed: 144 mph.
Ceiling: 18,500 ft.

Bell UH-1 Iroquois ("Huey")

Instantly recognizable to many Americans, especially to those who grew up watching Vietnam War footage on TV, the Bell UH-1 "Huey" is arguably the most successful helicopter ever developed. In a period spanning five decades more than 16,000 of these aircraft have been produced in two dozen models, for all branches of service and more than 40 foreign countries. Hueys were the most widely used helicopters in Vietnam, transporting men and supplies, but also serving in MedEvac, command and control, air assault and gunship roles.

Bell Aircraft's Model 204 prototype first flew in 1956 as part of a design competition to develop a new air ambulance for the US Army. Deliveries of the HU-1, the military's first turbine-powered helicopter, began in 1959. In 1962, just prior to its first deployment to Vietnam, the aircraft was redesignated as the UH-1 Iroquois. But Army pilots had already been calling it the "Huey" for some time, and the name stuck.

The UH-1 became the backbone of the Army's "flying cavalry" in Vietnam, delivering combat troops where needed, and evacuating the injured and the dead. Unarmed MedEvac Hueys ("Dust Offs") and lightly-armed troop carriers ("Slicks") were often escorted by special Hueys ("Hogs") outfitted with powerful machine guns and air-to-ground missiles. Beginning in 1967 Hog gunships were replaced by yet another version of the Huey, this one specifically designed as a gunship – the AH-1 Cobra attack helicopter.

Hueys were known for their ease of operation, impeccable maintenance record and durability on the battlefield. But they were also known for the unmistakable whap-whap sound of their twin rotors slicing through the air, which gave the enemy a two-mile warning of their approach. To mitigate this vulnerability Huey pilots in Vietnam developed "nap of the earth" flying techniques, skimming just above the jungle canopy and popping up at the last minute to strafe the surprised enemy at their listening posts.

The Huey on display at the Armament Museum is a UH-1M donated to the Air Force by the US Army. M-model Hueys were C-models fitted with more powerful engines and carrying specialized equipment, including low-light-level television and searchlights for night attacks.

Sources: 3, 14, 15, 16, 22, 25, 36, 43, 66, 78, 82, 83, 84, 85, 86

Length: 37 ft, 9 in.
Height: 11 ft, 8 in.
Wingspan: 38 ft, 11 in.
Empty Weight: 8,084 lbs.
Max Speed: 543 mph.
Ceiling: 47,500 ft.

Lockheed T-33 T-Bird

This two-seat version of the Lockheed F-80 Shooting Star was the only jet trainer in the US inventory from 1948 until 1957. A whole generation of cadets learned to fly in this aircraft. More than 6,000 T-33s were manufactured in ten years of production by the US, Canada and Japan, making it the most widely used jet trainer in the world and the most-constructed jet in American history.

Because the US Army Air Corps' first jet fighter, the P-80, was a single-seat aircraft, learning to fly it was a daunting, solitary prospect. An alarming number of planes and pilots were lost to inexperience. As a solution, the Shooting Star's manufacturer, Lockheed, tried to sell the idea of a tandem model – one seat for the student, one for the instructor. The Air Corps opposed the idea, saying they didn't want to "waste" any fighter airframes as they were in the midst of wartime production frenzy. Lockheed responded by developing the trainer anyway, using its own resources.

The dual-seat aircraft was created by extending the fuselage and canopy of a P-80B by three feet to accommodate an extra cockpit, complete with dual controls. It had a smaller fuselage fuel tank than the P-80, but the distinctive wingtip tanks were retained. Its air conditioning system was upgraded, and four of its six .50-caliber machine guns were removed. Otherwise it was the same aircraft, down to its single Allison J33 turbojet engine.

Finally convinced, the newly formed US Air Force awarded a contract for twenty of the new trainers in January 1948, to be designated the TF-80C. On March 22 the prototype made its first flight. And on May 5, its designation was officially changed to the T-33A Shooting Star (although the nickname "T-Bird" soon caught on).

The US Navy accepted 150 T-33s in 1948, but its high landing speed made it unsuitable for use on aircraft carriers. Lockheed developed yet another model, the T2V-1 Sea Star, which was able to land at lower speeds and came with an arrester hook for deck landings. The Navy would eventually purchase 700 Sea Stars, which were later designated the T-33B.

The T-33 became a bestseller around the world. Lockheed produced 5,691 of them in its US plants. Through licensing agreements, Canada and Japan produced hundreds more overseas. The Royal Canadian Air Force version, the Canadair CT-133 Silver Star, replaced the Allison J33 engine with a Rolls Royce Nene 10 turbojet. The Silver Star was in continuous service from the early 1950s until 2005. The Japanese version, made by Kawasaki, was called the Wakataka, or "Young Hawk."

By whatever name, the T-33 has served in the air forces of over thirty countries, and was imported in great numbers by France, Greece, Italy, the Philippines, Portugal, Spain, Taiwan, Thailand, Turkey, and West Germany. It was adapted for many uses besides pilot training. Many countries used it as a reconnaissance aircraft or as a light attack craft. In the US, many were assigned to units that flew the latest fighters, such as the F-101 Voodoo, where they towed target drones or served as mock targets, or "bogeys," themselves. Since the T-33 had a second seat that could accommodate a passenger, they were used through the 1960s by the Air Force's aerial acrobatic team, the Thunderbirds, as a VIP/press aircraft.

In the early 1960s the T-33 was gradually phased out as the Air Force's premier trainer in favor of the Cessna T-37 Tweet, which allowed instructors and students to sit side-by-side, and the Northrop T-38 Talon, the first supersonic trainer. But the T-Bird was still used in large numbers by the Air National Guard and many foreign countries for several more decades. The last T-33s were retired by the Air National Guard in 1987. At least fifty privately owned T-33s are in flying condition today.

The T-33A on display at the Armament Museum was built in 1955 in Lockheed's Burbank, California plant and was assigned to the 185th Fighter-Interceptor Squadron, Oklahoma ANG. Through the 1960s and 1970s it continued to serve with the ANG in Louisiana, Ohio, New Jersey and Vermont. Its last assignment was with the 325th Fighter Weapons Wing (TAC), at Tyndall AFB, Florida. It was donated to the Armament Museum in 1986.

Sources: 3, 7, 8, 30, 51, 52, 53, 66, 70, 81

Length: 43 ft, 5 in.
Height: 15 ft.
Wingspan: 33 ft, 7 in.
Empty Weight: 13,650 lbs.
Max Speed: 685 mph.
Ceiling: 44,500 ft.

Republic F-84F Thunderstreak

The Thunderstreak was the swept-wing successor to the rugged, straight-wing Republic F-84 Thunderjet, the US Air Force's first post-war fighter. The F-84 Thunderjet proved itself as a capable ground-attack aircraft in Korea, destroying enemy railroads, bridges and supply depots, but its speed and maneuverability were no match for North Korean MiGs in a dogfight.

Defense Department funds were short in 1949, but advances in swept-wing technology were so promising that Republic Aviation decided to develop the Thunderstreak using its own company resources. The first prototype flew in 1950, but it was much slower than Republic had hoped. The Air Force, by now interested in the project, suggested replacing the standard F-84 engine with a more powerful J65 turbojet. This necessitated heightening the fuselage by seven inches, streamlining the bubble canopy, and reducing the size of the air intakes. The new prototype attained a greater speed than the F-86H Sabre, the fastest American jet at the time.

The F-84F first went into service in 1954, and it became the first American jet exported in large numbers. Of the 2,711 Thunderstreaks produced, 1,301 were delivered to NATO countries. A reconnaissance version, the RF-84F Thunderflash, was also exported in large numbers. Like its predecessor, the F-84F was rugged, dependable, and an excellent ground-attack aircraft. It served the Air Force in that capacity until replaced by the supersonic F-100 Super Sabre in the early 1960s.

The F-84F was involved in some unusual projects during its career. One involved installing a turboprop engine and supersonic propeller in place of the aircraft's turbojet engine. The resulting aircraft was so noisy it was nicknamed the "Thunderscreech." In another experiment, escort Thunderstreaks were suspended as "parasites" from the bellies of huge B-36 bombers in an attempt to save fuel during bombing missions. In-flight refueling technology rendered that idea obsolete.

The Armament Museum's F-84F was delivered to the Air Force in 1954 and served in various Tactical Air Command units until 1962, when it was assigned to the Illinois Air National Guard. It was dropped from the active inventory in 1972 and came to the museum for display in 1979.

Sources: 2, 3, 6, 30, 66

Length: 37 ft, 6 in.
Height: 14 ft, 8 in.
Wingspan: 37 ft, 1 in.
Empty Weight: 11,125 lbs.
Max Speed: 685 mph.
Ceiling: 49,000 ft.

North American F-86 Sabre

America's first swept-wing jet aircraft, the F-86 was also arguably the first aircraft to break the sound barrier. On October 1, 1947, two weeks before Chuck Yeager made his famous flight in the Bell XS-1, test pilot George "Wheaties" Welch allegedly exceeded Mach 1.0 in a dive during a test flight in the prototype XP-86. Unfortunately for Welch, a measurement glitch made the flight "unofficial," and the feat went to Yeager.

The Sabre was originally designed with straight wings, and was very similar in appearance to the F-84 Thunderjet. The wings of the original Sabre were lifted straight from North American Aviation's famous propeller-driven plane, the P-51 Mustang, with the addition of wingtip fuel tanks. But German engineering data captured after WWII on the advantages of swept wings in high-speed flight led to a change in design. The first production model F-86 - with swept wings - flew on May 20, 1948. In September of that year an F-86 set a new world record of 670.84 mph, just a hair faster than Yeager's top speed in the Bell XS-1.

The aircraft's ease of handling was legendary. "It flew exceedingly well," remembers one retired F-86 pilot. "You could just about think what you wanted to do and let go of the control and the airplane would go ahead and do it just the way you wanted it to." Sabres were rushed to the front lines in Korea to take on the Soviet-built MiG-15 and regain air superiority. By the end of hostilities they had destroyed 792 MiGs, with the loss of only 76 Sabres, a 10-to-1 victory ratio.

More than 5,500 Sabres were built in the United States and Canada. The airplane was also used by the air forces of 20 other nations, including West Germany, Japan, Spain, Britain and Australia.

The F-86F displayed at the Armament Museum is a tribute to Captain Joseph C. McConnell of the 39th Fighter Interceptor Squadron, the leading American ace of the Korean War, who achieved triple-ace status with sixteen MIG-15 kills. It was donated to the museum by General Chok Young Bock of the Republic of Korea Air Force.

Sources: 3, 27, 66, 87, 89

Length: 47 ft.
Height: 15 ft, 6 in.
Wingspan: 38 ft, 10 in.
Empty Weight: 21,000 lbs.
Max Speed: 900 mph.
Ceiling: 51,000 ft.

North American F-100 Super Sabre

North American Aviation began development of a high-performance version of its successful F-86 Sabre in 1948. The new fighter was larger than the F-86, and was designed with wings sharply swept back at a 45-degree angle, a more powerful engine, a distinct oval air intake in the nose, and a unique slab tailplane set low in the fuselage.

The aircraft made its initial flight in 1953, breaking the world speed record at more than 750 mph. At the time it was the world's fastest jet fighter, with the possible exception of the Soviet MiG-19, then under development. It went into production a year later as the Super Sabre, the first Air Force fighter capable of cruising at supersonic speeds.

As the first aircraft of the so-called "Century Series" of fighters, the F-100 was nicknamed the "Hun," short for "Hundred."

Originally designed as an interceptor to destroy enemy aircraft in flight, "Huns" gained a reputation during the Vietnam War for their ability to deliver ordnance at high speed, taking out enemy bridges, road junctions and river barges. They were also important in high speed forward air control, or "Fast FAC," missions, which involved loitering for hours over enemy airspace, seeking out targets, such as surface-to-air (SAM) missile sites, for other fighter-bombers to destroy. Fast FAC missions were arguably the most dangerous job in the war.

F-100s equipped the USAF Thunderbirds aerobatic demonstration squadron from 1956 until 1968. After the Vietnam War, most Super Sabres were turned over to Air National Guard units, where they continued to be flown until 1979.

The F-100C displayed at the Armament Museum is depicted as the F-100F flown by Colonel (then Major) George "Bud" Day when he was shot down over North Vietnam in 1967. Day was the first commander of the Fast FAC squadron in Vietnam. During his six years of captivity, Day befriended a fellow POW, Navy Lieutenant Commander (later Senator) John McCain. Day later campaigned with his old friend during McCain's two bids for the White House. In 1976 Day was awarded the Congressional Medal of Honor. He still lives in the local area.

Sources: 2, 3, 30, 66

Aircraft Walking Tour
Air Force Armament Museum

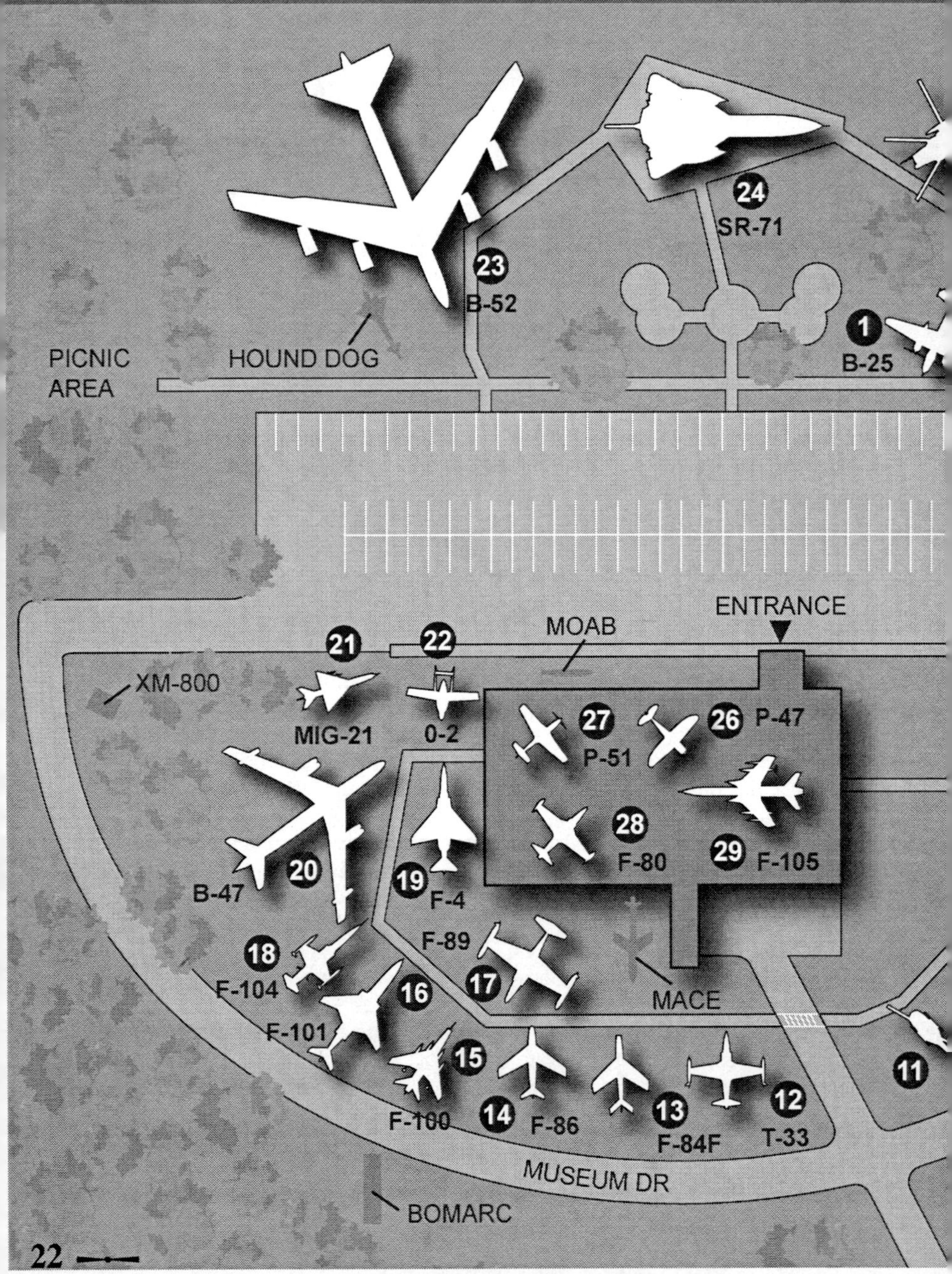

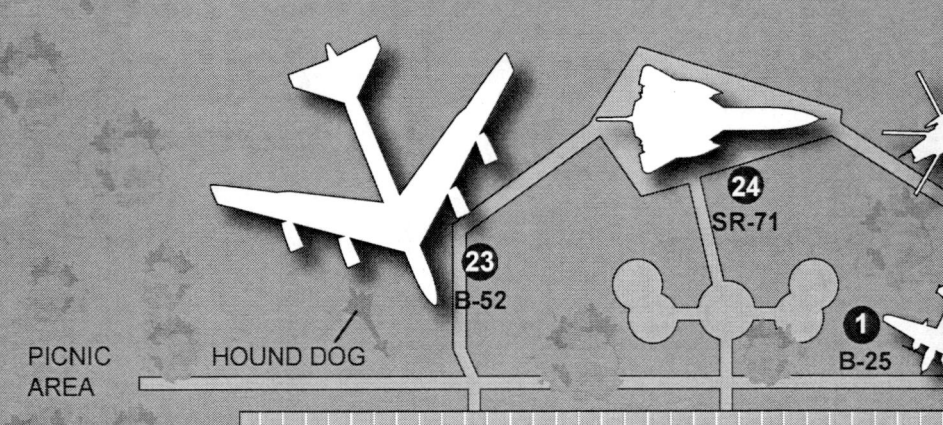

Length: 71 ft, 1 in.
Height: 18 ft.
Wingspan: 39 ft, 8 in.
Empty Weight: 28,500 lbs.
Max Speed: 1,095 mph.
Ceiling: 52,100 ft.

McDonnell F-101 Voodoo

The versatile F-101 served many roles during the Cold War. Originally designed as a long-range bomber escort, it was used as both a low-altitude fighter-bomber and high-speed interceptor, and ended up as the Air Force's first supersonic photoreconnaissance aircraft. At the time of its introduction it was the heaviest fighter ever built, and yet it was also the first aircraft capable of exceeding 1000 mph in level flight.

In the late 1940s the Strategic Air Command cancelled the production of McDonnell Aircraft's new XF-88 fighter. With the introduction of self-sufficient, high-altitude jet bombers like the B-52, SAC had decided long-range fighter escorts were no longer needed. But with the experience of Korea SAC changed its mind and ordered a redesign of the XF-88 to serve as an escort for the B-36 bomber. The resulting aircraft, designated the F-101 Voodoo, had twice the range and three times the engine power of its predecessor.

Although nicknamed the "one-oh-wonderful" by its fans, the F-101 was not without problems. Plagued with an intractable design flaw that caused it to pitch-up without warning at high speed, its large-scale production was delayed until 1957 as engineers agonized over a solution.

The Voodoo was extremely fast for its day and set numerous records, including a world absolute speed record of 1,207 mph on December 12, 1957. In the same year an F-101 set the New York to Los Angeles speed record of 3 hours and 7 minutes. Photoreconnaissance versions of the Voodoo were used during the 1962 Cuban Missile Crisis and during the late 1960s in Vietnam.

The Voodoo can be distinguished by its "T-tail" set high above the fuselage, out of the way of the exhaust from its twin jet engines, similar to a later McDonnell design, the F-4 Phantom II.

The F-101B was a two-seat bomber-interceptor version of the Voodoo, unique in being the first armed with nuclear-tipped Genie air-to-air missiles. The Armament Museum's F-101B was delivered to the Air Force in 1958. It served less than two years before it was returned to McDonnell Aircraft Corporation, to be modified for special tests. It was donated to the Armament Museum in 1979.

Sources: 3, 13, 30, 66

Length: 53 ft, 10 in.
Height: 17 ft, 6 in.
Wingspan: 60 ft, 5 in.
Empty Weight: 25,200 lbs.
Max Speed: 636 mph.
Ceiling: 49,200 ft.

Northrop F-89 Scorpion

The F-89 was a two-seat, twin-engine jet fighter/interceptor designed to locate, intercept, and destroy enemy aircraft by day and night under all types of weather. It was used almost exclusively in the far north to protect the US from the Soviet Union in the early years of the Cold War. Because it needed the ability to fly slowly when necessary in the harsh Alaskan weather, its manufacturer, Northrop, opted for straight wings and specialized ailerons, called "decelerons," that could be used as air brakes. The F-89 was the last Air Force fighter with a wingspan greater than the length of its fuselage.

The Scorpion, so named for its high, thin tail, carried a pilot in the forward cockpit and a radar operator in the rear who guided the pilot into the proper attack position. Beginning in 1950, the first three versions of the F-89 carried fixed wingtip fuel tanks and an armament of four 20mm cannons. By 1952, with the introduction of the F-89D, the cannons were eliminated and the wing tanks were replaced by wing pods each carrying 52 Mighty Mouse rockets. The unguided air-to-air rockets had a much greater range than cannon shells and were powerful enough to down an enemy bomber, but they had to be fired in large volleys in the hope that one would strike its target.

In 1956 the Scorpion became the first aircraft to carry the Hughes Falcon air-to-air heat-seeking missile, the USAF's very first guided missile. A year later, on July 19, 1957, a Genie test rocket was fired from an F-89J, the first time in history that an air-to-air rocket with a nuclear warhead was launched and detonated. The idea behind the Genie rocket was that the large blast radius caused by the nuclear explosion obviated the need for accuracy.

Northrup produced 1,050 F-89s for the US Air Force before they were phased out, beginning in 1957, and replaced by the F-102 Delta Dart. A few were still flown as late as 1969 by the Wisconsin Air National Guard. The Armament Museum's F-89D was manufactured in 1955. Converted to the J configuration two years later, it carried nuclear-tipped Genie rockets. It was donated to the museum in 1993.

Sources: 2, 3, 30, 66

Length: 54 ft, 8 in.
Height: 13 ft, 6 in.
Wingspan: 21 ft, 11 in.
Empty Weight: 12,760 lbs.
Max Speed: 1,320 mph.
Ceiling: 57,500 ft.

Lockheed F-104 Starfighter

With its long, tube-like fuselage and a ridiculously small wingspan of only 21 feet, the F-104 has often been called the "missile with a man in it." The aircraft was never popular with US pilots, and only 300 were produced for the Air Force. Of these, only 21 were F-104Ds, two-seat trainers like the one on display at the Armament Museum.

The Starfighter was designed by a team within Lockheed's secretive Skunk Works division, headed by famed engineer Clarence "Kelly" Johnson. The idea behind the design was the need for a high-speed, high-altitude air superiority fighter to take on the advanced Soviet MiGs encountered in Korea. Range was not so important, and was sacrificed for speed.

The result, first unveiled in 1954, was the world's first Mach 2 aircraft. In 1958 an F-104A set a world speed record of 1,404.19 mph. A year later a C-model Starfighter set a world altitude record of 103,395 feet, more than 3.5 times the height of Mt. Everest. The F-104 was the first aircraft to hold simultaneous official world records for speed, altitude and time-to-climb.

Lockheed strengthened the fuselage and wings in its later G-model and sold several hundred to NATO allies as a ground fighter. The new model was so popular that 1,600 were built overseas under license, where they remained in frontline service in several European and Asian countries well into the 1980s.

The US fleet of Starfighters was phased out in the 1960s, except for eleven aircraft destined for a special role with NASA. American astronauts trained in specialized NF-104As, which were rocket-assisted to boost them to heights above 120,000 feet. Starfighters were also used to test the durability of Space Shuttle heat shielding tiles. A company called Starfighters, Inc., based next to the Shuttle Landing Facility at the Kennedy Space Center, recently obtained five F-104s from Italy. They expect to turn a profit using their F-104s to conduct supersonic high-altitude instrument tests for the commercial space industry.

The F-104D on display at the Armament Museum was last flown at Edwards AFB, California, where it was used in the late 1960s in support of the X-15 spaceplane program. It was obtained by the Museum in 1986.

Sources: 2, 3, 24, 28, 30, 42, 65, 66

Length: 58 ft, 3 in.
Height: 16 ft, 6 in.
Wingspan: 38 ft, 5 in.
Empty Weight: 28,300 lbs.
Max Speed: 1,459 mph.
Ceiling: 59,600 ft.

McDonnell Douglas F-4 Phantom II

First developed in the 1950s as a carrier-based fighter for the US Navy, the two-seat, 25-ton F-4 would become the Air Force's most celebrated fighter over the course of the next two decades. The Phantom II was to Vietnam what the Sabre was to Korea. With its powerful twin turbojets it could carry twice the bomb load of the World War II-era B-17 at twice the altitude – flying at two times the speed of sound.

The Navy's carrier version of the F-4 first entered service in 1961 as a fleet defense interceptor. In competitions held between the Navy's new plane and the best Air Force fighters, the Phantom excelled in nearly every category, including speed, climb rate, radar detection and payload weight. Impressed, the Air Force envisioned the aircraft as its next generation air superiority fighter. With a few minor design changes, including widening the tires for use on tarmac instead of hard steel decks, the plane was ordered into production in 1962 as the F-110A, later redesignated the F-4C. In 1965 the first Air Force Phantoms were shipped to Vietnam.

The first F-4s in Vietnam had no guns. Instead each aircraft carried four Sidewinder heat-seeking missiles under its wings and four Sparrow radar-homing missiles in shaped recesses under its belly. The Sidewinders were very effective in a close tail-chase, but getting into position behind a highly maneuverable MiG-21 was no easy task. The AIM-7 Sparrow could destroy an enemy at a distance of over 25 miles, using powerful radar to steer itself toward its target at Mach 3.7. But at those distances the pilot couldn't always be sure the target was hostile. With the addition of the M61-A1 cannon and the perfection of aerial combat maneuvers like the barrel roll, F-4 pilots gained the upper hand over their North Vietnamese rivals, destroying more than 170 MiGs.

The F-4 was gradually replaced by F-15s and F-16s. By the time production ended in 1979 more than 5,000 had been built.

The Armament Museum's F-4C was built in 1964 and was last flown in 1986. In that same year it was transferred to the Armament Museum for static display.

Sources: 3, 29, 66, 72

Length: 107 ft, 1 in.
Height: 27 ft, 11 in.
Wingspan: 116 ft.
Empty Weight: 79,000 lbs.
Max Speed: 607 mph.
Ceiling: 38,850 ft.

Boeing B-47 Stratojet

The Stratojet was the first US aircraft specifically designed to deliver nuclear weapons, and the mainstay of the Air Force's nuclear deterrent force through the dangerous Cold War years of the 1950s. Sleek, fast, and gigantic for its time, the new bomber, powered by six turbojet engines slung on pods beneath razor-thin, swept-back wings, was unlike anything seen before. It was also difficult to fly, especially during landings. The Stratojet "was terribly unforgiving of mistakes or inattention," recalls one Air Force general. "Although often admired, respected, cursed, or even feared, the B-47 was almost never loved."

With the appearance of Nazi jets in 1944, the Army Air Forces spurred a competition to develop a jet-propelled bomber to counter them. Needed was a plane with the range of a bomber and speed of a fighter, one that could reach its target and return safely home without fighter escorts. Boeing's first attempts to meet this need were not successful, and the North American B-45 Tornado became the first US jet bomber. Not to be outdone, Boeing's engineers discarded their original plans and went back to work, utilizing captured German data on swept-wing technology.

The first experimental B-47 was revealed to the public on December 17, 1947, the same month that the United States Air Force was established, and 44 years to the day after the Wright brothers' first manned flight. Not since the B-17 Flying Fortress twelve years before had the roll-out of a new plane been so startling. It had ultra-thin, shoulder-mounted wings swept back at an amazing 35-degree angle. Its six General Electric J35 axial-flow turbojet engines were slung in pods beneath the wings. Its cockpit housed a crew of only three -- a pilot and copilot under a fighter-like bubble canopy, and a navigator hidden in a "dark space" in the nose. Since the key to its speed was the low drag of its thin, unencumbered wings, landing gear and fuel had to be housed in the fuselage. Its landing gear was a pair of two-wheel trucks placed for and aft on the fuselage centerline, with small outrigger wheels attached under two of the engine pods to provide stability on the ground.

On its first overseas deployment from Maine to Fairford, England, the Stratojet flew at an average speed of 575 mph, faster than most jet fighters of the day, making it literally invulnerable to attack for many years. While chasing a B-47 in a P-80 Shooting Star during early test trials, famous test pilot Chuck Yeager admitted he had to turn back because he couldn't keep up.

Designed for speed, the Stratojet could be difficult to control on take-offs and landings. To help the heavy bomber get off the ground, 33 jettisonable rockets of 1,000 pounds of thrust each were attached to its belly. The black smoke from the rockets made the B-47 appear to be on fire as it rose into the clouds. Even with the use of a large braking parachute, its high landing speed delayed the deployment of the B-47 as runways around the world had to be lengthened to accommodate it. Complicating matters was the plane's technological complexity. The crew of three had to keep track of more than 300 gauges, dials, switches and levers.

Boeing B-47E during rocket-assisted take off test (US Air Force)

The B-47 had completely replaced the propeller-driven bomber by 1955. There were 27 combat-ready B-47 wings in Strategic Air Command by 1956, each with its squadron of KC-97 refueling tankers. The ability to refuel in the air gave the Stratojet the intercontinental range it needed to ensure nuclear deterrence, a job it handled well during the darkest days of the Cold War, until replaced in the early 1960s by the B-52.

The aircraft on display at the Armament Museum was the last operational B-47 in the Air Force inventory, and one of only two RB-47Hs still in existence. The RB-47H was a specially modified B-47 that carried three additional crewmembers in a compartment added in place of the bomb bay. It would fly over enemy territory to spy on radar sites. While nearly all B-47s were retired by the late 1960s, the RB-47H continued for several years. It was finally dropped from the Air Force inventory in 1976.

Sources: 2, 3, 10, 24, 30, 33, 48, 66

Length: 51 ft, 9 in.
Height: 15 ft, 9 in.
Wingspan: 23 ft, 6 in.
Empty Weight: 11,460 lbs.
Max Speed: 1,300 mph.
Ceiling: 50,000 ft.

MIG-21 Fishbed

The proliferation of B-47s and B-52s during the early years of the Cold War was a frustrating challenge for the Soviet Union. They needed a plane that could fly fast enough and high enough to intercept US bombers, yet small and agile enough to serve as a frontline tactical fighter at lower altitudes. In 1955 the Mikoyan-Gurevich (MiG) Design Bureau produced both swept-wing and delta-winged prototypes. It was the delta-winged version that made its first public appearance at the Soviet Aviation Day display in June 1956 as the MiG-21. Popularly nicknamed "Balalaika" for its resemblance in plan view to the Russian stringed musical instrument, NATO gave it the less romantic codename "Fishbed."

The MiG-21F (Fishbed-C) was the first full-scale production version. It is easily distinguished from later models by its partially obscured nose cone, which would be lengthened in subsequent models to house search-and-track radar. The Fishbed-C was armed with a single 30-mm cannon and two underwing pylons on which were typically mounted K-13 Atoll heat-seeking missiles. The MiG-21 was capable of Mach 2 speeds like its rival fighters, the F-105 Thunderchief and F-4 Phantom, but its small size and light wing-loading gave it the advantage of tighter turns – a big advantage in a dogfight.

But experience won out over maneuverability to give US pilots in Vietnam the advantage in aerial combat against North Vietnam's agile MiG-21s. F-4 Phantom aces such as Colonel Robin Olds mastered maneuvers such as the high-speed barrel-roll to turn the tables on the MiGs and send heat-seeking Sidewinder missiles up their tailpipes.

More MiG-21s have been produced than any other supersonic fighter in history. In 30 years of production more than 13,000 were built for the air forces of more than 56 countries, including countries friendly to the United States. It has taken part in nearly every armed conflict since Vietnam, and around 3,000 are still operated today by the air forces of more than 40 countries worldwide.

The Armament Museum's first-generation MiG-21 Fishbed-C is appropriately displayed near its nemesis, the F-4C Phantom II. It is painted in the Soviet camouflage paint scheme of its time.

Sources: 3, 24, 29, 62, 63, 80

Length: 29 ft, 9 in.
Height: 9 ft, 5 in.
Wingspan: 38 ft, 2 in.
Empty Weight: 2,800 lbs.
Max Speed: 199 mph.
Ceiling: 19,300 ft.

Cessna O-2 Skymaster

The unorthodox Cessna Skymaster appears somewhat out of place among fighter jets. Few realize the important role this unassuming aircraft played during wartime. As one of the primary Forward Air Controller (FAC) aircraft during the Vietnam War, the O-2 was assigned the task of loitering slowly over enemy positions and identifying targets for American attack jets. The experienced pilots chosen for these dangerous missions were some of the most decorated veterans of the war.

"There was a valid reason to have all FACs be qualified tactical fighter pilots," said one former wartime FAC. "In Vietnam, almost every bomb dropped and every rocket fired from an aircraft had been cleared by a FAC. He ran the air war on the battlefield, coordinating all air strikes, the weapons to be used, and their employment. His was the responsibility to make sure that no friendly troops were hurt by the air strikes .... In short, you bombed where the FAC told you to, and if he said 'no,' then you didn't bomb."

Underestimating the need for FACs in the years following the Korean War, the Department of Defense only began development of a dedicated FAC aircraft after the Vietnam conflict was well underway. In the meantime, there was a desperate need for them. In 1964 the Army transferred its fleet of single-engine L-19 liaison airplanes to the Air Force. Renamed the O-1 Bird Dog, it served as the primary FAC aircraft in Vietnam until the O-2 Skymaster replaced it in 1967.

A military adaptation of the Cessna Model 337, the O-2 had two engines and two propellers, one pulling and another pushing. The rear engine was situated behind the cockpit, between twin tail booms. Having two in-line engines would allow the plane to operate normally if one was disabled. High wings allowed the crew an unobstructed view.

The O-2 was phased out with the introduction of the OV-10 Bronco in 1969. The Museum's O-2 served active duty as a FAC in Vietnam from 1968 through 1970. It was donated to the Museum in 1988. It is painted black in the color scheme of O-2s flying night FAC missions.

Sources: 3, 19, 20, 21, 66, 67, 88, 90

Length: 160 ft, 11 in.
Height: 40 ft, 8 in.
Wingspan: 185 ft.
Empty Weight: 168,500 lbs.
Max Speed: 634 mph.
Ceiling: 47,000 ft.

Boeing B-52 Stratofortress

One of history's most successful weapons systems, the B-52 Stratofortress is the only aircraft in the world with eight jet engines. It is capable of dropping or launching the widest array of weapons in the US inventory. It served through the 1960s and 1970s as the Air Force's flagship high-altitude, high-speed, long-range heavy bomber and reconnaissance aircraft.

The original Boeing design in 1946 had straight wings and six turboprop engines. Jet engines consumed too much fuel to meet the range requirement for the planned long-range bomber. But by 1948, turbojet technology had advanced enough to make their use practicable, and the B-52 was completely redesigned. With eight jet engines mounted in pairs on a wing with a 35-degree sweep, the prototype had a maximum speed greater than 600 mph when it first flew in 1952. The fighter-type cockpit of the prototype was later eliminated because General Curtis LeMay believed that side-by-side seating of the pilot and the copilot would ensure better communication between crewmembers.

A total of 744 B-52s were built for the Air Force between 1953 and 1962. Beginning in the late 1950s they began to replace the B-47 as Strategic Air Command's primary nuclear deterrent aircraft, carrying two AGM-28 Hound Dog nuclear missiles on wing pylons. These missiles had a range of more than 600 miles, allowing "standoff" launches hundreds of miles from the target, thus reducing the risk to the launch aircraft.

B-52s played important roles during the Vietnam War. Modified B-52Ds, known as Big Bellies, dropped aerial mines in North Vietnamese harbors and river inlets. During the Gulf War in 1991, B-52s from Barksdale AFB, Louisiana flew 35 hours nonstop to Iraq and back, in the longest strike mission in the history of aerial warfare. Dozens of B-52s are still in service today and are expected to continue in use until 2040.

The aircraft displayed at the Armament Museum is a B-52G, distinguished by its shorter (by eight feet) vertical stabilizer. The wings of this model were sealed and used to store fuel. This particular aircraft flew to Iraq out of Barksdale AFB during Operation Desert Storm.

Sources: 3, 48, 66

Length: 107 ft, 5 in.
Height: 18 ft, 6 in.
Wingspan: 55 ft, 7 in.
Empty Weight: 59,000 lbs.
Max Speed: 2,250 mph.
Ceiling: 85,000 ft.

Lockheed SR-71 Blackbird

The SR-71 is an Air Force variant of the CIA's secretive Mach 3, high altitude, aerial-reconnaissance aircraft, the A-12 OXCART. Capable of flying literally at the speed of a rifle bullet at an altitude of more than 85,000 feet, it remains, more than forty-five years after it was first developed, the fastest and highest-flying manned aircraft ever built.

The OXCART project got its start in 1958, only two years after the CIA began overflights of Soviet territory with its U-2 reconnaissance aircraft. The U-2 was designed to fly at 70,000 feet, which in the mid-1950s was thought to be beyond the range of Soviet radar detection and missile defenses. But technology was advancing rapidly, and the U-2 was tracked on Soviet radar from its first flight. A radically new aircraft was called for, one that could fly higher and faster than anything yet conceived.

The A-12 (and later, the SR-71) was designed and built at Lockheed's top-secret "Skunk Works" facility in Burbank, California. To maintain secrecy, all components of the first Blackbirds were hand-made on site. Flight-testing began in 1962 at Nevada's Groom Lake test facility, later made famous as "Area 51." To get the aircraft to the Nevada desert undetected, it was shipped in pieces on flatbed trucks in huge crates. The two-day trip was conducted under police escort. Trees and road signs had to be cut down to allow passage of the strange convoy.

The key to the Blackbird's speed was the conical "spikes" thrusting forward from its twin turbojet engines. As the aircraft accelerated, the spikes retracted, allowing compressed, superheated air to be mixed with gas and fed to the afterburners. The specialized jet fuel combusted at 3,400 degrees F., very close to the maximum temperature possible for hydrocarbon fuels. The release of energy was tremendous to behold, as if "the Devil himself were blasting his way straight from Hell." The Pratt & Whitney J58 was the most powerful air-breathing propulsion device ever made. Each one produced enough thrust to power the world's largest ocean liners.

Despite the extreme cold temperatures at an altitude of 85,000 feet (nearly three times higher than the summit of Mt. Everest), the friction from sustained flight above Mach 3 produces temperatures over 1000 degrees F. on some aircraft surfaces. Over 90 percent of the SR-71's body is composed of a special heat-tolerant titanium alloy, nearly as strong as steel but half its weight. At the height of the Cold War, titanium was difficult to obtain. It is a beautiful bit of irony that much of the metal needed to produce the CIA's most secretive spy-plane was obtained covertly – from the Soviet Union.

During flight the cockpit was literally as hot as an oven. Pilots were protected by a pressurized flight suit with an independent oxygen supply, similar to an Apollo space suit. The suit was also useful in the extreme cold and sudden depressurization of a high-altitude bailout, assuming the air blast during ejection didn't kill the pilot instantly. If he did survive, he would enjoy a seven-minute, twelve-mile freefall before the jerk of his main chute detached him from his seat.

The "Big Tail" in flight (US Air Force)

In 1976 an SR-71 set two world records that still hold today – an official speed record of 2,193.167 mph and an altitude record of 85,068.997 feet. But these records were set under normal operating parameters. During high performance tests in 1965 these aircraft reached speeds as high as Mach 3.29 (over 2,200 mph) and altitudes over 90,000 feet. To put the speed of the SR-71 into perspective, during one trial in 1974 a blackbird flew from London to Los Angeles in 3 hours and 47 minutes. It literally outraced the setting sun, landing some four hours before the time of day it took off.

The Armament Museum's Blackbird is the largest SR-71 in existence, owing to the nine-foot extension protruding from her aft fuselage. In 1975 this aircraft was chosen as the test platform for a new surveillance camera and electronic countermeasures (ECM) suite, which was contained in the nine-foot boom. Flight tests confirmed there were no significant performance problems with the added technology, but the ECMs did not show increased protection from incoming missiles. The project was canceled. The "Big Tail," as this aircraft is called, is the only one ever produced.

Sources: 3, 35, 38, 44, 49, 66, 73, 74, 76, 77

Length: 88 ft.
Height: 25 ft.
Rotor Diameter: 72 ft.
Empty Weight: 32,000 lbs.
Max Speed: 165 mph.
Ceiling: 16,000 ft.

Sikorsky MH-53 Pave Low IV

With a main rotor spanning 72 feet and with the strength to lift 38 fully equipped troops, the MH-53 Pave Low was the largest, most powerful and most technologically advanced helicopter ever flown by the US Air Force. Designed to conduct long-range, low-altitude missions to insert, extract, and resupply special operations forces, these fearsome machines were involved in nearly every contingency, covert or otherwise, from Vietnam to Iraq. The Pave Low fleet numbered only 72 aircraft, but their combined combat record includes 140 Silver Stars, an average of nearly two Silver Stars per airframe over a 40-year career.

The MH-53 Pave Low was one variant of the H-53 family of helicopters developed by Sikorsky Aircraft in the 1960s in response to developments in Vietnam. The largest and heaviest helicopter ever built by the American military, the H-53 was designed for the transportation of equipment, supplies and personnel.

A specialized Air Force version of the H-53 entered service in Vietnam in 1967 to augment the HH-3 "Jolly Green Giant" helicopter in combat search and rescue (CSAR) missions. Nicknamed the "Super Jolly Green Giant," the HH-53 was faster and had nearly three times the takeoff weight of the HH-3. It was equipped with armor plating, self-sealing fuel tanks, three 7.62mm miniguns, and could transport 22 litter patients and four medics. Its 250-foot external rescue hoist could lift 20,000 pounds.

Super Jollies made headlines many times in the 1970s. In 1970, after top-secret training at Eglin AFB, HH-53s were involved in an unsuccessful raid into North Vietnam to rescue prisoners-of-war from the Son Tay prison camp. In 1975 these aircraft were used in an operation to rescue the crew of the freighter *Mayaguez* from Cambodian Khmer Rouge pirates. And in 1978 Super Jollies were sent to Guyana to recover bodies after the "Peoples Temple" mass suicide incident.

Meanwhile, a secret program was underway to convert the HH-53 into a CSAR vehicle that could operate in total darkness and in adverse weather. Codenamed Pave Low, the program delivered its first HH-53H Pave Low III in 1979. Equipped with forward-looking infrared sensors, Doppler radar navigation, and terrain-following/terrain-avoidance radar, the Pave Low III could fly clandestine, low-level missions in any weather, day or night.

In 1986, additional enhancements were made, including a cockpit with blue-green lighting for use with night-vision goggles, modern GPS navigation, more powerful engines, and heavier armor. Reclassified as "special operations" aircraft, the refurbished MH-53J ("M" for "multi-use") became a mainstay of the Air Force Special Operations Command (AFSOC), and participated in nearly every conflict and humanitarian relief effort of the 1990s. The MH-53J served in the invasion of Panama and saw extensive service during the Gulf War, where it was used to insert special operations teams deep in the Iraqi desert to hunt for "Scud" missiles.

A final upgrade in the 1990s, "Pave Low IV," added the latest in computer technology to the already sophisticated machine. A moving digital map now gave the crew instant access to the total battlefield situation, including threats over the horizon. Once a threat was detected, the computer would recommend the best course of action.

The MH-53M Pave Low IV opened the air war in Operation Desert Storm, flew reconnaissance missions over Ground Zero in the immediate aftermath of the September 11th attacks, and was continuously deployed in support of the Global War on Terrorism. AFSOC's entire fleet of MH-53s was retired in 2008 and its important CSAR role is now performed by the V-22 Osprey tiltrotor aircraft.

Pararescuemen do a "fast rope" from a hovering HH-53 Super Jolly Green Giant (US Air Force)

The Pave Low IV on display at the Armament Museum is the most recent addition to the facility and the only aircraft to actually arrive under its own power. Manufactured in 1974, it was serving at Eglin AFB in 1978 when it became part of the recovery team sent to Jonestown, Guyana, to evacuate the bodies of more than 900 Americans who committed suicide under the influence of cult leader Jim Jones. It underwent conversion to the Pave Low configuration in 1979 and was assigned to the 1st Special Operations Wing (SOW) at Hurlburt Field in 1980. It saw active duty with special forces troops in Bosnia and Iraq. Its last assignment was with the 16th SOW in 1995.

Sources: 3, 32, 34, 37, 40, 46, 56, 58, 59, 60, 61, 66

Length: 36 ft, 1 in.
Height: 14 ft, 2 in.
Wingspan: 40 ft, 9 in.
Empty Weight: 11,000 lbs.
Max Speed: 433 mph.
Ceiling: 42,000 ft.

Republic P-47 Thunderbolt

The P-47 was the largest, heaviest, and most numerous single-engine US fighter in World War II. Pilots loved it because they felt safe behind its thick armored plating and self-sealing fuel tanks. They also enjoyed the feeling of being ensconced in a spacious, comfortable cockpit. "Like sitting in a lounge chair," was the description that has come down to us. P-51 Mustang pilots, who had to endure long flights in cramped conditions, used to joke that P-47 pilots avoided enemy fire by running around inside the cockpit.

The heft of the P-47 developed out of a necessity to fit the new 2,000-hp Pratt & Whitney 18-cylinder radial engine and its 12-foot-2-inch four-blade propeller onto an existing airframe. In 1940, Republic Aviation had sold its P-43 Lancer, a much smaller fighter, to the US military, but news coming out of Europe made it clear that the allies would need something much more robust if they ever hoped to take on the German Luftwaffe.

The result, the XP-47B Thunderbolt, first flew on May 6, 1941. It hardly resembled the P-43. The fuselage had been greatly extended and angled upward on spindly legs. The sophisticated landing gear was designed to retract in length and fold itself into the wing so room was left for the ammunition feeding its eight .50-caliber Browning machine guns. A turbosupercharger was mounted under the rear fuselage to allow the plane to retain horsepower at high altitudes. Even without the ammunition for its guns, the Thunderbolt weighed six tons. Fully armed with bullets and bombs it exceeded eight.

When it first arrived in England toward the end of 1942, US pilots were skeptical. They were used to flying British Spitfires and Hurricanes, which weighed about half as much. Thunderbolts climbed slowly, looked eerily similar to German Focke-Wulf 190s (which could be dangerous in the heat of a dogfight) and "dove like bricks." Its shear bulk compelled one pilot to declare the P-47 a "Juggernaut." Forever after it was known as the "Jug."

Soon pilots realized their Jugs could outdive all opposing fighters, which gave them a huge advantage in aerial combat. Its heavy airframe, armored plates, and powerful engine made it "the roughest, toughest fighter of the war." It became the favorite of many pilots. One fighter group chose to continue flying Thunderbolts when most others had switched to the more maneuverable P-51 Mustang. The two leading American aces in Europe flew only P-47s.

When rocket launchers and bomb pylons were added to the underside of the wings, beneath its heavy machine guns, the plane was transformed into a formidable ground attacker. And when external fuel tanks were added in place of bombs, it became an effective escort for heavy bombers headed deep into Germany.

More than 15,600 Thunderbolts were built during the war, more than any other fighter. By mid-1943, the three Republic Aviation factories were running at full capacity. By the close of the war, the P-47 had flown half a million sorties and had destroyed 11,874 enemy aircraft, 9,000 locomotives, 86,000 railway cars, 6,000 armored fighting vehicles, and 68,000 trucks.

About midway through the production run of the D-Model P-47, the "greenhouse" canopy surrounding the cockpit was replaced by a bubble canopy, greatly improving pilot visibility. Both the "razorback" and "bubbletop" varieties continued to be used throughout the war, often flying side-by-side in the same squadron.

After the war the P-47 was gradually phased out, along with other propeller-driven fighters, in favor of jet aircraft. Thunderbolts were still used by some Air National Guard units as late as 1954.

The Thunderbolt displayed at the Armament Museum is a P-47N named *Expected Goose,* as its nose art graphically reveals. The N-Model can be distinguished from other P-47s by its squared wingtips and long "strake," or stabilizing ridge, running from behind the bubble canopy to the tail fin. The N-Model was designed as a long-range version of the P-47 for use as a bomber escort in the Pacific theater during WWII.

There are only about 60 surviving P-47s in the world today. Only a dozen or so are in flying condition, and nearly all of them are the more common D-Model. *Expected Goose* is a very rare example of a flight-worthy P47N.

Sources: 2, 3, 64, 66, 87, 89

Length: 32 ft, 3 in.
Height: 8 ft, 8 in.
Wingspan: 37 ft, 10 in.
Empty Weight: 7,125 lbs.
Max Speed: 437 mph.
Ceiling: 41,900 ft.

North American P-51 Mustang

In 1944, the Truman Committee, a group of senators convened to root out waste in war spending, concluded that the P-51 Mustang fighter was "the most aerodynamically perfect pursuit plane in existence." Widely regarded as "the fighter that won the war," and praised by its pilots as the "Cadillac of the skies," the Mustang was considered by many to be the greatest fighter of WWII.

In response to Nazi aggression in the 1930s, Great Britain undertook an expansion of its Royal Air Force. They placed an order for Curtiss P-40 Tomahawks in the US, but Curtiss couldn't make them fast enough. In desperation, a British purchasing commission asked a competitor, North American Aviation, if they could open their own production line for P-40s. They could not, responded NAA; but they could design a new fighter that would be better than the P-40.

NAA's P-51 prototype was first flown at the end of October 1940. It was a sleek craft with a distinctive intake scoop under the center fuselage, which housed the radiator for the 1,150-hp Allison V-1710 engine. They had designed the aluminum skin of the aircraft to exacting specifications. Rivets and fasteners were installed flush with the wings and fuselage, reducing drag to negligible levels. The protruding radiator intake served dual duty as a thruster, expelling excess engine heat through its narrow rear nozzle. The combination of low-drag wings and extra thrust from its radiator gave the Mustang a speed advantage over other fighters at lower altitudes.

The P-51 excelled as a reconnaissance and ground-attack aircraft. But above 15,000 feet it was outperformed by other RAF fighters, such as the iconic Spitfire. The Mustang was thus relegated to low-level duty in both the British and American air forces; that is, until 1942, when British engineers had the clever idea of putting the Spitfire's Rolls-Royce "Merlin" engine, with its two-stage supercharger, into a P-51. The wedding of the Merlin with the Mustang would dramatically change the course of events through the rest of the war.

By this time the Merlin engine was being built under license in the US by the Packard Motor Car Company. Packard-built V-1650 Merlins now became standard in new P-51s.

The performance improvement was astounding. In tests the new Mustang reached a speed of 433 mph and an altitude of 40,600 feet. With the addition of disposable fuel tanks under the wings and a new internal tank behind the cockpit, its range was also dramatically improved. By March 1944, the first Mustangs appeared over Berlin escorting B-17 heavy bombers. In the Pacific theater they escorted B-29s to Japan from Iwo Jima.

Through the remainder of the war, the Mustang was the scourge of the Luftwaffe and the bane of the Mitsubishi Zero. By war's end they had destroyed more than 5,000 enemy aircraft, more than any other fighter.

Crew Chief Staff Sgt. Anthony Belesi cuts open dry K-rations huddled under a canopy blanket beneath the Wing of his 7th Air Force P-51 fighter on Iwo Jima. Mechanics remained on the flight line 14 hours from dawn to dark with no shelter. (US Air Force)

Nearly 15,000 Mustangs were built during the war. Renamed the F-51 in 1948, Mustangs were still used as fighters during the Korean War, but were eventually phased out in favor of jet aircraft. They were flown by the Air National Guard through the 1950s, and used by many foreign militaries as late as 1984. They are still one of the fastest propeller-driven aircraft around, and can be seen at air shows and races around the world.

Before WWII, Ford Motor Company struck a deal to build Merlin engines for Rolls-Royce. At the last minute, Henry Ford rescinded the offer. Being an isolationist, he refused to support someone else's war. He would build engines or airplanes for the defense of his own country, he said, but not for Great Britain. A quarter of a century later, Henry's company paid indirect homage to the Merlin by naming its new line of youth-oriented coupes after the P-51 Mustang.

In the late 1960s the Defense Department contracted with Cavalier Aircraft Corporation to create new Mustangs for export to foreign militaries. Cavalier produced eleven F-51Ds under this contract, from bits and pieces of surplus airplanes, nine of which were given to Bolivia. The remaining two became US Army chase planes. The Cavalier aircraft displayed at the Armament Museum, built in 1968, was used as a chase plane during testing of the Lockheed Cheyenne helicopter.

Sources: 3, 18, 50, 64, 66, 68, 89

Length:
Height: 14 ft, 8 in.
Wingspan: 57 ft, 6 in.
Empty Weight: 25,000 lbs.
Max Speed: 450 mph.
Ceiling: 45,000 ft.

Lockheed F-80 Shooting Star

The F-80 was America's first combat-ready jet fighter. It came late on the scene during the Second World War. So late, in fact, that it missed the war entirely. But it made history nonetheless, taking part in the world's first all-jet air battle, setting a world speed record, and becoming the first US aircraft to exceed 500 mph in level flight.

The Germans were the first to test a jet-powered aircraft, the Heinkel He-178, in the summer of 1939. Luckily for the Allies, the Nazi leadership preferred to invest in proven piston-powered craft rather than waste resources on new technology, and the arrival of the Messerschmitt Me-262 was delayed for several years. In the meantime, the British were developing their own turbojet capabilities. Their efforts would eventually result in the Gloster Meteor, the only jet fighter fielded by the Allies during the war.

The Americans were late in developing jet power because they were keenly focused on supplying the Allies with top-quality propeller-powered fighters, including the Mustang and Thunderbolt. US factories were turning out huge numbers of these planes, each of them equipped with turbosuperchargers that allowed them to fly efficiently at ever-higher altitudes. Ironically, the technological principle behind the supercharger was very similar to what was required to run a turbojet engine.

In April 1941, Chief of the US Army Air Corps, Major General Henry "Hap" Arnold, witnessed the first flight of a British turbojet prototype, the Gloster E.28/39. Soon, three of the engineers who had helped develop the British engine were on their way to the US, recruited by Arnold to help his own engineers catch up. On October 1, 1942, a Bell Aircraft test pilot became the first person to fly a jet on American soil when he lifted off briefly from Rogers Dry Lake, California, in the XP-59A, prototype of the P-59 Airacomet.

Sixty-six P-59 Airacomets were ordered and built, but they were never able to show an improved performance over their propeller-driven counterparts. A new jet fighter was needed, one that could hold its own with the planes the Nazis were beginning to build.

In May 1943 the USAAF asked Lockheed to manufacture an experimental airframe to be powered by a British jet engine. Lockheed began work on the XP-80 even before the contract was signed in October. The work progressed in complete secrecy, with engineers working around the clock in a temporary building away from prying eyes. The project was so secret that many of the company's own executives were kept in the dark. This was the origin of Lockheed's famous "Skunk Works" division.

Three-aircraft formation of Lockheed F-80Bs (US Air Force)

The XP-80 made its maiden flight on January 8, 1944. The P-80 Shooting Star was introduced to the public on August 1, 1945 in a screaming display in front of 150,000 spectators at a Wright Field air show. Later that summer, thirty Shooting Stars were crammed aboard an aircraft carrier and sent to the Philippines for the final assault on Japan. Unfortunately, someone had failed to pack some crucial equipment required to get the jets airborne, and they sat waiting on the deck for more than a month, just long enough to miss the end of the war.

America's first operational jet still set records and inspired a generation of pilots. Before becoming the first man to break the sound barrier, Chuck Yeager trained in a P-80. He said that flying jets was "like trying to learn how to ride a race horse after riding only on elephants." On June 19, 1947 Colonel Albert Boyd set the world absolute speed record piloting a modified P-80 at more than 623 mph.

Although originally intended to be a high-altitude interceptor, the F-80 (the "P" for Pursuit was changed to an "F" for Fighter in 1948) was used extensively as a fighter-bomber in the Korean Conflict, primarily for rocket, bomb, and napalm attacks against ground targets. On November 8, 1950, an F-80C flown by Lt. Russell Brown, flying with the 16th Fighter-Interceptor Squadron, shot down a Russian-built MIG-15 in the world's first all-jet-fighter air battle.

Only 1,731 F-80s were produced. They were quickly superseded by faster, swept-wing jets like the F-84F Thunderstreak and the F-86 Sabre. There is not a single F-80 in flying condition today, although many are on static display around the world. The last combat-capable F-80 was grounded by the Uruguayan Air Force in 1975.

Sources: 2, 3, 51, 53, 66, 91

Length: 64 ft, 5 in.
Height: 19 ft, 8 in.
Wingspan: 34 ft, 11 in.
Empty Weight: 26,850 lbs.
Max Speed: 1,390 mph.
Ceiling: 51,000 ft.

Republic F-105 Thunderchief

Nicknamed the "Thud" or "Lead Sled," the F-105 was the heaviest, fastest, and most complex single-engine fighter-bomber in history when it was first unveiled in 1955. The largest model could carry 14,000 pounds of ordnance aloft, three tons more than the WWII-era B-17 Flying Fortress. During the air war over North Vietnam in the late 1960s, the Thud flew more missions and took heavier losses than any other aircraft.

In 1951 Republic Aviation began a private project to develop a supersonic tactical fighter-bomber to replace its F-84F Thunderstreak. The new design called for a single-seat air-superiority fighter with a unique internal bomb bay that could deliver conventional or nuclear bombs at high speeds and low altitudes in any weather. The prototype aircraft broke the sound barrier on its first flight and was ordered into production as the F-105 Thunderchief in 1958.

The Thud was distinguished by forward-pointing air intakes and low-mounted, swept tailplanes. The unique air intakes were designed to provide a double shockwave at supersonic speeds, to slow the air entering the compressor to an acceptable velocity. The single Pratt & Whitney J75 engine could produce 24,500 pounds of thrust, propelling the Thunderchief to speeds above Mach 1 at sea-level or Mach 2 above 40,000 feet.

The F-105 was the primary strike aircraft in North Vietnam from 1965 until 1970. Flying fast and low, it destroyed scores of heavily defended targets, but in the process exposed itself to a growing number of enemy surface-to-air missile (SAM) sites. More than 380 Thuds were shot down during the war, representing over 20 percent of the US Air Force's total fixed-wing losses. Faster, two-seat F- and G-model F-105s were introduced in 1966 and 1967 to participate in "Wild Weasel" missions. These new aircraft were armed with Shrike anti-radiation missiles designed to seek out and destroy enemy antiaircraft radar sites.

The F-105D on display inside the Armament Museum's main building spent its entire career stateside and is thus one of the few to survive the Vietnam War unscathed. It was transferred from Andrews AFB, Maryland to Eglin AFB in 1981 and delivered to the Museum for static display in 1985.

Sources: 2, 3, 24, 30, 66

List of Sources

1. "A-10 Warthog Battle Damage Repair – Desert Storm 1991." *2951st Combat Logistics Support Squadron*. Retrieved Nov 29, 2011. <http://www.2951clss-gulfwar.com/statistics.htm>
2. Aeronautical Systems Center, History Office, Air Force Materiel Command, Air Force History and Museums Program, United States Air Force. *Splendid Vision, Unswerving Purpose: Developing Air Power for the United States Air Force During the First Century of Powered Flight*. Wright-Patterson Air Force Base, Ohio: United States Air Force. 2002.
3. Air Force Armament Museum, Eglin AFB, Florida. Accession records.
4. "Airpower Classics: B-17 Flying Fortress." *Air Force Magazine*. Feb 2006: 96. Retrieved 3 Mar 2011. <http://www.airforce-magazine.com>
5. Aleshire, Peter. *Eye of the Viper: the Making of an F-16 Pilot*. Guilford, CT: The Lyons Press, 2005.
6. Apple, Nick P. and Gene Gurney. *The Air Force Museum*. Third Revised Edition. New York: Crown Publishers, 1980.
7. *Aviastar*. Retrieved 15 Dec 2011. <http://www.aviastar.org/air/usa/lok_t-33.php>
8. *Aviation History*. Retrieved 13 Oct 2011. <http://www.aviation-history.com/lockheed/p80.html>
9. "B-25 Mitchell Bomber." *Boeing*. 2012. Retrieved 8 Feb 2012. <http://www.boeing.com/History/>
10. *B-47 Stratojet Association*. Retrieved 1 Jul 2011. <http://www.b-47.com/preserved/b04296/b04296.html>
11. "B-57 Still Going Strong at 59." NASA. 3 Sep 2003. Retrieved 14 Nov 2011. <http://www.nasa.gov/>
12. Baugher, Joseph F. "General Dynamics/Grumman F-111A." *Joebaugher.com*. 23 Dec 1999. Retrieved 29 Nov 2011. <http://www.joebaugher.com/usaf_fighters/f111_1.html>
13. Baugher, Joseph F. "McDonnell F-101A Voodoo." *Joebaugher.com*. 12 Aug 2001. Retrieved 13 Sep 2011. <http://www.joebaugher.com/>
14. "Bell Helicopter Pocket Guide: Bell UH-1Y." *Bell Helicopter*. 2011. Retrieved 19 Oct 2011. <http://www.bellhelicopter.com>
15. "Bell UH-1 Iroquois (Huey) Multi-Role/Utility/Attack/Transport Helicopter." *Military Factory*. Retrieved 24 Oct 2011. <http://www.militaryfactory.com/>
16. "Bell UH-1M Iroquois Huey." *Combat Air Museum*. Retrieved 24 Oct 2011. <http://www.combatairmuseum.org/aircraft/bellhueyuh1m.html>
17. "Birth of the 'Spectre' Gunship." *Spectre Association*. 2008. Retrieved 19 Jan 2012. <http://www.spectre-association.org/historySpectre.htm>
18. "Business: Ford's Rolls-Royces." *Time Magazine*. 8 Jul 1940. Retrieved 23 Sep 2011. <http://www.time.com/time/magazine/article/0,9171,795076,00.html>
19. Butler, Jimmie H. "USAFA's Forward Air Controller Heritage." *Checkpoints Magazine*. Dec 2007: 72-74. Retrieved 31 Oct 2011. <http://memwall.usafalibrary.com/>
20. "Cal Fire Aviation Management History." *California Department of Forestry and Fire Protection*. Retrieved 30 Oct 2011. <http://www.fire.ca.gov/about/about_aviation_history.php>
21. "Cessna O-2 Super Skymaster." *Warbird Alley*. 2006. Retrieved 30 Oct 2011. <http://www.warbirdalley.com/o2.htm>
22. Chiles, James R. *The God Machine*. New York: Bantam Dell, 2007.
23. Cox, Bob. "For Lockheed Martin's F16, a dwindling list of likely buyers." *Fort Worth Star-Telegram*. 29 May 2011. Retrieved 18 Dec 2011. <http://www.mcclatchydc.com/2011/05/29/114949/for-lockheed-martins-f16-a-dwindling.html>
24. Dick, Ron. *Reach and Power: the United States Air Force in Pictures and Artifacts*. Washington, D.C: United States Government Printing Office, 1997.
25. Everett-Heath, John. *Helicopters in Combat: the First Fifty Years*. London: Arms and Armour Press, 1992.
26. "F-15K Slam Eagle for the Republic of Korea." *Boeing*. Retrieved 8 Jan 2012. <http://www.boeing.com>
27. "F-86 Sabre: Air Superiority Over Korea." *History Chanel*. Retrieved 13 Apr 2011. <http://www.history.com/shows/dogfights/videos>
28. "F-104." *Federation of American Scientists*. Retrieved 12 Sep 2011. <http://www.fas.org/nuke/guide/usa/airdef/f-104.htm>
29. Franks, Norman. *Aircraft Versus Aircraft: the Illustrated Story of Fighter Pilot Combat Since 1914 to the Present*. London: Grub Street, 1999.
30. Fredriksen, John C. *Warbirds: an Illustrated Guide to U.S. Military Aircraft, 1915-2000*. Denver: ABC-CLIO, 1999.
31. Gething, Michael J. *Modern Fighting Aircraft: F-15*. London: Salamander Books, 1983.
32. Getlin, Noel. "Last Flight for the Pave Low Near Shalimar." *Eglin Dispatch*. 5 Sep 2008. Retrieved 7 Oct 2011. <http://rotorheadsrus.us/documents/>
33. Goebel, Greg. "B-47 Variants." *Vectorsite*. 1 Jul 2010. Retrieved 13 Oct 2011. <http://www.vectorsite.net/avb47_1.html#m1>
34. Goebel, Greg. "Sikorsky S-64 & S-65." *Vectorsite*. 1 Mar 2011. Retrieved 17 Oct 2011. <http://www.vectorsite.net/avskbig_1.html#m5>
35. Graham, Richard H. *SR-71 Revealed: the Inside Story*. Osceola, WI: MBI Publishing, 1996.
36. "H-40." *Global Security*. Retrieved 24 Oct 2011. <http://www.globalsecurity.org/>
37. "H-53/Sikorsky S-65 Family." *Global Security*. Retrieved 7 Oct 2011. <http://www.globalsecurity.org/>
38. *Habu*. "61-7959." Retrieved 13 Jan 2012. <http://www.habu.org/sr-71/1795>
39. Heppenheimer, T.A. "The Jet Plane is Born." *American Heritage*, Vol 9, Issue 2. Fall 1993.
40. "HH-53 Super Jolly Green Giant." *Global Security*. Retrieved 7 Oct 2011. <http://www.globalsecurity.org/>
41. Hillaker, Harry. "Tribute to John R. Boyd." *Code One Magazine*. July 1997.
42. *International F-104 Society*. Retrieved 20 Jun 2011. <http://www.i-f-s.nl/>
43. "Iroquois (Huey) History." *Global Security*. Retrieved 24 Oct 2011. <http://www.globalsecurity.org/>
44. Jacobsen, Annie. "The Road to Area 51." *Los Angeles Times*. 5 Apr 2009. Retrieved 10 Jan 2012. <http://www.latimes.com/>
45. Johnsen, Frederick A. "The Making of an Iconic Bomber." *Air Force Magazine*, Vol. 89, No. 10, Oct 2006. Retrieved 17 Oct 2011. <http://www.airforce-magazine.com/>
46. Johnson, Lauren. "PAVE LOW dedicated into AF Armament Museum." *Air Force Special Operations Command*. 10 Sep 2008. Retrieved 3 Sep 2011. <http://www.afsoc.af.mil/news>
47. Kaplan, Robert D. "Rereading Vietnam." *The Atlantic*. 2007. Retrieved 15 Aug 2011. http://www.theatlantic.com/magazine/
48. Knaack, Marcelle Size. *Encyclopedia of U.S. Air Force Aircraft and Missile Systems, Volume II: Post-World War II Bombers, 1945-1973*. Washington, DC: Office of Air Force History, 1988.
49. Kucher, Paul R. "Lockheed SR-71 Blackbird." SR-71 Online. 2010. Retrieved 22 Jan 2012. <http://www.sr-71.org/blackbird/sr-71/>
50. Leffingwell, Randy. *Mustang: 40 Years*. St. Paul, MN: Crestline, 2003.